First published 1991 in *Greek Myths*
by Walker Books Ltd, 87 Vauxhall Walk, London SE11 5HJ

This edition published 2017

2 4 6 8 10 9 7 5 3 1

© 1991, 2006, 2017 Marcia Williams

The right of Marcia Williams to be identified as author/illustrator of this work
has been asserted by her in accordance with the Copyright, Designs and Patents Act 1988

This book has been typeset in Goudy Old Style

Printed and bound in Great Britain by Clays Ltd, St Ives plc

British Library Cataloguing in Publication Data:
a catalogue record for this book is available from the British Library

ISBN 978-1-4063-7159-8

www.walker.co.uk

# The Twelve Tasks of Heracles

## &

## Arion and the Dolphins

# Marcia Williams

WALKER BOOKS

AND SUBSIDIARIES

LONDON · BOSTON · SYDNEY · AUCKLAND

# Contents

## The Twelve Tasks of Heracles

## Arion and the Dolphins

# The Twelve Tasks of Heracles

# Part One
## The Story of Heracles

Heracles was born in Ancient Greece. He was the son of a mortal woman named Alcmene and the great god, Zeus. He was a tough, merry little baby, loved by almost everyone. Only Hera, Zeus's wife, hated him as he reminded her that her husband was not always entirely faithful.

One night, in a fit of jealousy, Hera sent two snakes to kill baby Heracles as he slept

in his cradle made out of an upturned shield. Heracles watched the deadly serpents as they crept under his bedroom door and slithered across the floor. As the snakes lifted their heads to strike Heracles, he grabbed them both by the neck and strangled them – he was just ten months old!

"No trouble," he gurgled, waving the snakes about as if they were mere toys.

Hera was furious

that her plan had come to nothing. She decided that the best thing to do would be to ignore Heracles.

"I'll just pretend he doesn't exist, the horrid little brat," she snarled.

As Heracles grew up, he became stronger and stronger. Not only was he a match for any wild beast, but he was also learned and wise. He married the woman he loved and they had many children.

"How many was it at the last count, dear?" he would teasingly say to his wife.

It seemed that Heracles's life was blessed, which did not please Hera, who was unable to resist keeping a jealous eye on him. She would look down from Mount Olympus, see his smiling face and scowl with displeasure.

"This happiness has gone on long enough!" snapped Hera one day. "It must end – once and for all!"

That night, Hera cast a cruel spell on Heracles. He rose from his bed and – as though in a dream – he lashed out with his sword, slaying imaginary enemies. Only when

he woke, did he see that he had killed his own children.

His wife could not believe her beloved Heracles could do such a thing.

"Get out of here, you murderer!" she yelled.

Heracles was heartbroken and went to the

temple to seek forgiveness. The priestess
told him that he could only make amends
by serving his old enemy, King Eurystheus
of Mycenae.

"You must do twelve tasks for Eurystheus,
then the gods will forgive you," she said.

## Part Two
# The Twelve Tasks

## The First Task: The Nemean Lion

With a heavy heart, Heracles made his way to the court of King Eurystheus. The king, who was terrified of Heracles, jumped and hid inside a great big pot when he heard him approaching.

"Don't let him come too close," Eurystheus cried to his guards.

"I've got my orders," said
Heracles. "I'll do twelve
things for you and no more!"

"With a bit of luck you'll
be dead after the first one,"

muttered the king from inside his pot.

"I doubt it," said Heracles, who had yet to
be defeated by man or monster.

"Your first task is to kill the Nemean lion,"
chuckled the king, sure that Heracles would
soon be lion's meat.

The Nemean lion had a hide so thick
that no sword or arrow could penetrate it,
but Heracles was undeterred. He travelled
to the Valley of Nemea, where he waited
patiently outside the lion's den. At sunset
the beast returned from its latest killing spree.

The lion was a terrible sight indeed, spattered with blood and dragging a sheep's carcass behind him. Heracles fired an arrow, but it glanced straight off the lion's shoulders.

Alerted to Heracles's presence, the lion dropped the sheep and leapt towards him. Heracles tried to hit it with his club, but the club broke in two. He wrestled with the lion, and was all but overcome by its vast strength.

Finally, Heracles managed to get his arms around the beast's neck and, closing them

tighter and tighter, he slowly squeezed the life out of the fearsome creature.

"Ha!" said Heracles in triumph. "I always wanted a lion cloak!"

## The Second Task: The Lernean Hydra

When Heracles returned to King Eurystheus, wearing the lion as a cloak, the king nearly fainted in his pot.

"Oh, go away!" he cried.

"Not until you give me another task," replied Heracles.

So Eurystheus told Heracles to go and kill the many-headed hydra, whose breath could overpower any living creature. It lived in swamp land and guarded the Fountain of Amymone, preventing the villagers from getting fresh water.

Trying hard not to breathe, Heracles approached the hydra with his sword and a burning torch. As soon as he chopped off a

head he burned the stump, so that the hydra was unable to grow a new one. This worked until there was just one head left – an immortal head!

"So, you think you're strong do you, Mr Immortal?" scoffed Heracles.

"Strong enough for you!" replied the head.

"That's what you think!" laughed Heracles, lifting up a great boulder and squashing the life out of the last – and no longer immortal – head!

# The Third Task: Diana's Deer

When Heracles returned to King Eurystheus, stinking of swamp and hydra-breath, the king refused to put his nose outside the pot, but gave his orders from deep inside.

"Capture the goddess Diana's sacred, golden-horned deer and bring it back unharmed," hissed the king, crossing both fingers and toes in the hopes that Heracles would never return.

Heracles set off for the Arcadian Forest and waited by the Temple of Diana for her deer to appear. The deer was as quick as the wind and so elusive that many people wondered if it really existed. Eventually, Heracles caught sight of it, only for it to take fright and run as soon as it saw him. Heracles, who was also fleet of foot, chased it through the forest, over rivers, across borders and up mountains.

For a whole year, Heracles pursued the deer

relentlessly until one day he found himself back at Diana's temple. Only then did the deer appear to tire. Heracles was just about to sneak up and capture it when Diana herself appeared before him.

"You must not touch my deer, Heracles," she said. "Return to King Eurystheus and tell him what has happened. He will understand that your task has been completed."

## The Fourth Task: The Erymanthian Boar

So Heracles returned to court, much to King Eurystheus's displeasure.

"Your fourth task is to catch the savage Erymanthian boar, but I hope it kills you first. Its tusks can pierce any armour, so it probably will," chortled the king. "Especially as you have to bring it back alive!"

Heracles hitched up his lion cloak and set off for Mount Erymanthus, where the boar lived. After much hunting, he found it hiding in a snowdrift.

"I know you're in there, but how do I get you out alive?" Heracles pondered.

Eventually, with ropes and a great deal of muscle-power, Heracles had the boar trussed up and on his shoulders. He marched in triumph back to Mycenae, where he lifted

the lid of King Eurystheus's pot and popped the boar inside!

"Surprise!" laughed Heracles, slamming down the lid.

You might suppose that the boar would have killed the king and so put an end to Heracles's tasks, but it was not to be. The boar was as frightened of Heracles as King Eurystheus was, so the unlikely pair snuggled up together in the safety of their pot!

# The Fifth Task: Cleaning the Stables of King Augeas

With much coaxing, Heracles persuaded the king to poke his head out of the pot for long enough to tell him his fifth task.

"Why do you keep coming back?" moaned the king. "I wish you'd vanish into a pile of dung!"

Hoping his wish might come true, Eurystheus told Heracles to clean out the vast and filthy stables of King Augeas – in one night.

When Heracles saw the state of the stables, which were piled waist-high with horse dung, he realized that it was no job for a pitchfork. Undaunted, he built a dam that changed the direction of a nearby river. The river poured through the stables, washing them clean. Luckily for Heracles, the horses did not get washed away!

"I'm not just a muscle man, I've got brains too!" he grinned.

# The Sixth Task:
# The Stymphalian Birds

King Eurystheus did not grin when Heracles arrived back at court with his fifth task completed.

"I need to think up something deadlier," he growled.

So for his sixth task, the king sent Heracles to destroy a flock of man-eating birds, which lived in a dangerous swamp.

The king imagined the birds pecking over Heracles's bones and smiled to himself.

Unfortunately for King Eurystheus, those poor birds never got anywhere near Heracles's flesh, let alone his bones! Heracles shook a rattle to scare the birds out of the reeds, then shot them down like flies with poisoned arrows!

"Your birds m'lord," Heracles said to King Eurystheus, as he marched back into court with the birds held aloft.

# The Seventh Task: The Cretan Bull

The seventh task King Eurystheus set Heracles was to capture the marauding, fire-breathing bull of Crete – the terror of every islander.

"If nothing else, it'll singe your eyebrows," muttered the king.

Arriving on the island of Crete, Hercules hid

in the bushes and waited for the bull to approach. He grabbed the beast by the horns and held it fast until finally it was overcome by his strength and endurance.

Impressed by Heracles's power, the bull became as docile as a lamb and even gave his captor a ride on its back across the sea and all the way back to Mycenae – eyebrows still intact! Of all the tasks Heracles ultimately completed, this one would prove to be his favourite.

# The Eighth Task: The Horses of Diomedes

King Eurystheus was beginning to think he would spend the rest of his life hidden in his pot!

"Maybe, just maybe, the flesh-eating horses of Diomedes, the King of Thrace,

will defeat you," he said, more
wishing than believing.

However, after arriving in
Thrace, Heracles had little
trouble capturing the beasts. It seemed he
was invincible! Even when he was attacked
by a band of King Diomedes' men he was not
defeated. He captured the whole lot of them
and returned, with horses and men, to King
Eurystheus. The king was horrified.

"Take them away before they eat me!" he
screamed from his pot.

# The Ninth Task: The Girdle of Hippolyte

"Maybe the warrior-women of the Amazon and their queen will defeat you," said King Eurystheus, hopefully. "Fetch me the magic golden girdle worn by Queen Hippolyte," he continued. "I hear she's a match for any man!"

So Heracles crossed the Black Sea to the country of the Amazons and anchored his ship in their harbour. Queen Hippolyte rowed out

to greet Heracles, for she had heard many stories of his strength and bravery. Full of admiration, she made him a present of her belt.

This angered some of her warrior-women, who attacked Heracles, but he brushed them off as if they were merely annoying gnats. He was soon far off across the sea, the precious golden girdle glittering in the sunshine as he secured it around his waist.

# The Tenth Task: Cattle of Geryon

The tenth task that King Eurystheus set
Heracles was to seize the cattle of the
monster Geryon, which were guarded by
his two-headed dog, Orthrus. Geryon himself
had three bodies, three heads, six legs, six
arms and a pair of wings!

"Surely this task will be the end of you,"
sighed the king.

Upon reaching the island where Geryon
and his cattle lived, Heracles climbed to the
top of a mountain to find where they were
grazing. As he scanned the valley below,
Heracles was suddenly attacked by Orthrus.
Taking up his great club, he dispatched the
snarling beast from the top of the mountain,
over a cliff and out into the sea! The next

minute, Heracles was attacked by Geryon's herdsman, and he too was sent hurtling down the mountainside!

Heracles immediately set out to find the cattle and round them up, but as he began to herd them towards the boat, Geryon himself appeared swinging clubs from all six hands! Taking one of his poisoned arrows, Heracles felled the great giant before he could get close enough to do any harm and continued on his

way, with the cattle, back to King Eurystheus.

"Is it really you again?" sighed the king, hunkering down into the very bottom of his pot.

## The Eleventh Task: The Golden Apples

For his eleventh task, King Eurystheus decided to send Heracles all the way to Africa, to fetch the golden apples that grew in the Garden of the Hesperides.

"Hopefully Africa will swallow you up!" muttered the king.

The apples could only be picked by the giant Atlas, who was kept busy holding up the world, but Heracles wasn't worried. He travelled to Africa, overcoming dragons

and sea-gods on the way. When he finally
reached the garden, Heracles offered to hold
up the world for Atlas, if he would pick the
apples.

"I can probably hold it up with one hand,"
boasted Heracles.

"Anything for a rest," replied the giant,
handing the world to Heracles.

Atlas picked the apples and then, seeing
a chance to escape, he offered to take them
to King Eurystheus. Heracles agreed but,
sensing a trick, he asked Atlas if he would

take back the world – just for a second – while
he scratched an itch. So Atlas balanced the
world back onto his shoulders and the next
thing he knew Heracles had vanished into the
distance – without so much as a thank you!

"I've been duped," muttered Atlas, "and I
didn't even get to eat an apple!"

# The Twelfth Task: Cerberus!

By the time Heracles reached the court of King Eurystheus with the apples, he was getting tired of his adventures.

"I've been working for you for ten years," he grumbled, "and I'm getting fed up!"

"You're fed up," replied King Eurystheus. "What about me? I'm much too old to live in a pot. Fortunately for both of us there is only one task left."

The last task was the most dangerous of all: to fetch the king of the underworld's three-headed guard dog, Cerberus, from Hell itself. Even Heracles raised an eyebrow, for no one returned from the underworld alive. Nevertheless, down he went into the mouth of Hades armed only with his club and his

lion cloak. He crossed the River Styx and journeyed into the very heart of Pluto's kingdom.

Pluto was so surprised by his brave visitor that he agreed to lend him Cerberus, on the condition that he capture the dog without a weapon which, of course, Heracles did!

"After we have visited nice King Eurystheus,

I'll return you to this charming place,"
Heracles promised the slobbering beast.

When Heracles led Cerberus into court,
King Eurystheus shook so violently that his
pot nearly fell over!

"Poke your nose out one last time," said
Heracles.

"No way," replied Eurystheus. "Get out of

here once and for all – and take that growler with you!"

So Heracles sent Cerberus back to Hades and returned back home to his temple.

"I think the gods might now forgive you for

killing your children, Heracles," conceded the priestess. "You seem to have done quite well."

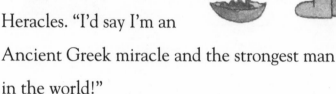

"Quite well?" exploded Heracles. "I'd say I'm an Ancient Greek miracle and the strongest man in the world!"

"Harrumph," said Hera, who was watching from her throne on Mount Olympus. "It never pays to be too sure, not while I've still got my eye on you…"

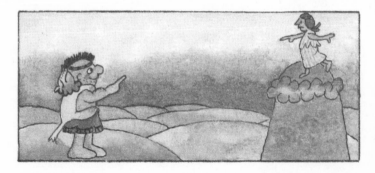

# Arion and the Dolphins

# Chapter One
# King Periander's Musician

Like most Greeks, King Periander of Corinth was a music-lover. His court bustled with singers, dancers and musicians, and music was everywhere.

"I do like my daily quota of music. Without it, I am just not myself," the king was fond of saying.

Some days, King Periander would call for soft, gentle music and on others he would tap his toes to fast dance music. Occasionally, he would have melancholy days when only sad music suited him, but there was never a day when the music of his favourite musician, Arion, did not give him pleasure.

Arion was a poet who played the lyre and sang. His wonderful voice and sweetly plucked

lyre were guaranteed to make King Periander feel at peace with the world. So when Arion asked permission to leave the court and travel to Sicily to take part in a music festival, King Periander was not at all pleased.

"I would be out of humour all the time you were away," he declared gloomily. "No. I can't and won't be without you. Don't even think about it."

But Arion couldn't stop thinking about it.

He thought about all the prize money he might win; he thought about how famous he might become; he thought about all the fans who might cheer and applaud him. So he plucked his lyre and sang softly to the king.

"Dear King Periander, If you let me go to Sicily, I promise I will win many prizes and bring great wealth and recognition to the court of Corinth. You and I will be famous the whole world over. Tralala!"

King Periander was not amused.

"That may be," snapped the king. "But your music is so sweet to my ears that I cannot imagine a single day without it."

"Know that I will return to you with the greatest haste, bearing the victor's crown," promised Arion.

"Oh, very well," sighed Periander. "But make sure you win every single contest and return with unimaginable speed. I will expect a share in every gram of gold that you win!"

# Chapter Two
# Fame and Fortune

So, when a ship had been manned and rigged, Arion set sail for Sicily. All the way there, he sat at the stern playing his lyre to the sailors and to the dolphins that danced through the ship's foamy wake.

Once in Sicily, it seemed that Arion could not play or sing a wrong note. All of the other musicians stared at him in amazement.

Audiences rose to their feet and cheered every time Arion picked up his lyre or opened his mouth to sing. Women threw flowers and swooned. Wealthy men did everything they could to persuade Arion to leave the court of Corinth and play for their own households.

Best of all, Arion won every single competition and the judges gave him top marks. Arion could not have been more delighted!

"I'm not just a star, but a megastar! I should return to Corinth before my head grows too big for my body!" he joked.

Arion imagined King Periander's delight when he saw all the riches he was returning with. It took twelve porters to carry his prizes

to the ship. The sailors' eyes glinted as they carefully stowed the boxes in the ship's hold.

"A nice bit of gold to line our purses!" they said. "We'd never have to work again if this lot was ours."

The sailors were rogues, each and every one, and they decided to steal Arion's prizes.

# Chapter Three
## The Thieves Show No Mercy

The sailors took it in turns to creep down into the hold and drool over Arion's hoard of riches. Every time they saw the array of prizes, they grew more and more determined to steal Arion's treasure.

When the ship was far out to sea, the thieving old salts whipped out their knives

and surrounded him.

"Your gold and your life!" they cried.

"Oh, show me some mercy," begged Arion. "Take my gold and spare my life."

"Shall we let him live?" the sailors asked themselves.

"No! He's safer dead. A dead Arion can't track us down … or tell of our evil deeds!" they cheered.

The sailors generously agreed to let Arion sing one final song, before they stabbed him and threw his body overboard. He

took up his lyre and knelt on the prow, where he sang to the gods to look on him kindly. As his last

sweet note drifted away, Arion threw himself into the sea. The startled sailors stared down over the railings, but the waves had closed over Arion and he was nowhere to be seen. The ship and the sailors sailed on, leaving Arion to his briny fate.

# Chapter Four
# Dolphins to the Rescue

Poor Arion was not a good swimmer. He sank deeper and deeper beneath the surface of the sea, until a school of dolphins that had been attracted by his singing took pity on him. They raised him to the surface and carried him back towards the shores of Corinth.

The dolphins swam with such speed that

Arion arrived home before the ship. He rushed straight to court, to tell King Periander of his adventure.

"You do smell a bit fishy!" grumbled the king, who was delighted to have his favourite musician back really – with or without his prizes. "To think I might never have heard you play again thanks to those rogues! I'll get my revenge – they will suffer for this! At least you've still got your lyre. Before you get washed and dried, you might just play me a song or two!"

# Chapter Five
## The Punishment

When the sailors arrived back in Corinth, King Periander hid Arion behind a screen and then summoned the rogues to court.

"Have you any news of Arion?" King Periander asked in an innocent voice.

"Why, yes," the sailors replied. "He has been delayed in Sicily by all the festivities. He was such a star – he just couldn't get away. He asked us to tell you that he will be returning as soon as he possibly can."

As they spoke these words, Arion appeared from behind the screen.

"I am not only a star, but I am a *live* star!" he smiled.

The sailors looked at Arion in horror! They tried to make a run for it, but the king's guards surrounded them.

"Shall we feed them to the fish or roast them for dinner?" King Periander asked Arion, for he was determined to see the murderous thieves executed.

"I don't think I could play a note after eating that lot," said Arion, turning slightly green.

Arion was more merciful than the king

and begged that the sailors be allowed to
live. King Periander, who would have done
almost anything to please his favourite musician, banished the sailors to an ugly, barbarous
land far from Corinth and spared their lives.

"And don't forget, you are banished for life!" he growled at the departing scoundrels.

"Don't just stand there! Fetch your lyre!" the king ordered, turning happily to Arion. "Those dolphins rescued you for a reason and that reason was to play for me!"

King Periander settled back to enjoy Arion's music. He closed his eyes and his thoughts grew calm. For the first time since Arion's departure, King Periander felt at peace with the world.

# Other fabulous retellings by
# *Marcia Williams*

978-1-4063-6279-4

978-1-4063-6272-5

978-1-4063-6276-3

978-1-4063-6273-

978-1-4063-5694-6

978-1-4063-5695-3

978-1-4063-5693-9

978-1-4063-5692-2

# Available from all good booksellers